Colorado

*mind*

Sunrise on the Maroon Bells–Snowmass Wilderness   GALEN ROWELL

# introduction

I came to love Colorado one snowbound night in Nebraska. A springtime blizzard, called in those parts an Alberta clipper, sailed south across the Great Plains. The savage weather closed the flat-land interstate highway. Hundreds of storm-stranded travelers hunkered in motels in prairie villages like Kearney, Gothenburg, and Grand Island.

I sat among the marooned as the winds howled and the snow piled higher, and Colorado became my dream land. What I missed most about my home state came clearly into focus.

The next day I saw one of my dreams come true. The storm moved east. The interstate reopened. I headed west. Close to Julesburg the roadway was clear of snow and the cruise to Denver was carefree. It was March, the sun was brilliant, the sky was a cloudless crystal blue. A few miles on, cresting a hill, I caught a glimpse of the snow-covered Rockies stretching across the western horizon.

No matter how many years I've lived in the Rocky Mountains, seeing them after being away is like seeing them for the first time. There is a freshness to that sight that stirs the soul.

That first view of the Rockies is something most travelers will always remember. Back in the gold rush days of the 1850s and 1860s, as prospectors neared the mountains, excitement grew with every step, bringing them closer to their dreams of wealth. Pikes Peak or Bust! "Mountain rises above mountain" wrote one of those argonauts, "peak above peak from the foothill westward in the distance, their summits white with snow and the peaks fairly touching the clouds, presenting a picture which few having seen can ever forget."

Standing on the Colorado prairie, I find it impossible not to think about all those who crossed these trails before us, most of them passing in the last dozen decades or so. Arapaho Indians hunting buffalo. Trappers seeking Bent's Old Fort. Plains-weary prospectors tramping west. Army troopers chasing Indians. Freight wagons. Railroad builders. Homesteaders and ranchers. A Model-T Ford from Kansas loaded with tourists. Interstate highway builders. Dam builders, irrigators, gas and oil prospectors.

Those prospectors of decades past never knew about plate tectonics. It's likely they cared little about glaciation, or worried about orogenices (or how the Rockies were formed). What caught their attention was the glint of gold, and the ores rich in silver. In a frenzy, they came to places like Central City, Idaho Springs, Cripple Creek, Leadville, and Creede. Dozens of Colorado communities tell the tale of mines cut into mountains, and men becoming millionaires.

I know an old-timer who is still "sitting on a gold mine," as he calls it. Over the last four decades he has twice struck it rich and become wealthy beyond his dreams. Twice he's had the bad luck to lose his fortune. Now he's older, a bit wiser, yet his eyes still sparkle with the optimism of youth. "It's got forty, maybe forty-five million worth of gold," he says, "if only I can get some investment to get the mine working."

Coloradans crave adventure, but they tend to be realists. They may be dreamy-eyed and euphoric while standing on top of a mountain, but they know life at the higher elevations has its limits.

A friend of mine named Pete is one of those realists. Maybe he's just a typical, old-fashioned Coloradan. He was born and raised in Estes Park. His father was an immigrant.

Coming after a generation of homesteaders who already had a head start, Pete's father had to buy his land to start a ranch. He did well at ranching, married the daughter of a local resort owner, and kept adding land to his personal empire.

Pete grew up helping his dad on the ranch, and helping his mother run a resort. Later he made a modest living selling real estate to the steady flow of latter-day settlers moving into Colorado. Today Pete is retired. So what is he like?

He's friendly. If there is one main characteristic you can attach to most Coloradans, it is their willingness to welcome you like a long-lost cousin. Maybe that's a frontier tradition, born out of loneliness: strangers are quickly made to feel at home.

He's self-reliant. He may be friendly, but he doesn't expect to feed and fuel the universe. He attributes his personal success to long hours, sacrifice, and hard work. He expects no less of others.

He's curious. He's a country boy at heart, but he's no hayseed. He's well educated. He's politically active and well-read. He talks to everyone, enjoys a good argument, and is willing to change his mind if he can be convinced. At the same time, he has strong opinions and isn't afraid to express them.

He's proudly provincial. He's been known to wear western style clothing. For special events and to impress Easterners, he wears a tattered cowboy hat. He can spin a yarn about the old days better than most. He likes to exaggerate, especially when talking to tourists, and rarely tells a story the same way twice.

Wranglers near Aspen   BRIAN BAILEY

He's slightly eccentric. For better or worse, Coloradans pride themselves in sounding (and sometimes acting) independent, especially in business and politics. The freedom of the frontier lives on. So Pete enjoys being unpredictable, just like a horse sometimes takes to bucking—simply for the kicks. Such actions can come as a surprise to his friends, but for Pete it's merely restlessness. He's a free spirit, hard to corral.

Finally, whether he admits it or not, he's an environmentalist. His entire life has been spent in the out-of-doors. He's a hiker and a horserider. He loves the mountains. Winter finds him cross-country skiing. The older he gets, the more passionate he becomes about protecting the land and its wildlife for the next generation. That's Pete. And that's old-fashioned Colorado.

Even though Pete's affection for Colorado is obvious, it is rarely expressed. He's not what we'd call a booster. But in thinking the Rockies are the best place to call home, Pete is not alone.

There are a growing number of people who quickly proclaim that Colorado is paradise. If ever there were a superlative-slinging contest, Colorado's latest arrivals could easily triumph over Texans. The mountains are "awesome," the skiing conditions are "fantastic," the scenery is "breathtaking," the wild rivers and wildlife are "amazing," and even the local sports teams are "incredible." Each year there are hundreds more who adopt Colorado as their home.

Typical of those newcomers is a friend of mine, whom I'll call Jim. After years of hard work with a big corporation in the midwest, he finally decided to "pull the plug," as he called it, and made his move to Colorado.

In previous years Jim vacationed here, taking annual ski trips to Copper Mountain, Breckenridge, and Steamboat Springs. Soon he started spending his summer vacations here, sampling places as diverse as Denver and Durango, Canon City and Glenwood Springs.

Now he's settled in one of Colorado's small towns. The pace of life is relaxed. Jim's Colorado home, nestled in a grove of ponderosa pine, tells him he's living in the middle of the western wilderness. No longer does he commute two hours a day to work. No more does he spend time standing in lines. No longer is he merely a face in the crowd. No traffic noise keeps him awake at night.

Like many newcomers, Jim worried at first about the winters here and bought a four-wheel-drive truck. After a year he sold it. He discovered the winters are milder than those of the midwest. Now his greatest fear is hitting a deer or elk as he rambles along the mountain roadways. Sometimes he frets about those same deer and elk (or is it rabbits or raccoons?) eating his newly planted shrubs and flowers.

Jim has played so much golf in the last few years that he's started to tire of the sport; now he spends more time with photography. He's enamored with the local scenery and talks endlessly about the wild creatures he's seen, most recently a mountain lion. His pet project this year is to photograph a favorite scene each month of the year, chronicling nature's changes. He's developed other new hobbies, too, including birdwatching, gardening, and hiking.

Now that he lives in a small town, there are numerous clubs and churches recruiting Jim for membership. Not too surprisingly, and considering his frame of mind, he joined the Optimists Club. He also volunteered to run the Chamber of Commerce information desk on Sunday afternoons. He's so well-informed and excited about his adopted town that he spends hours giving vacationers hints about places to stay, things to see or do, and the best places to eat.

That's Jim. In the tradition of the old west, he's definitely a booster. And he applauds Colorado in all seasons.

Colorado is a timeless place; it tests our definitions of time and place. The high country and vast landscape diminish the importance of almost every human enterprise. Cities, highways, suburbs, and whole counties shrink into insignificance. Political divisions make no impression—the moods and rhythmns of nature govern here. How boring it must be to live in a place where the weather never changes. Colorado's skies can deliver thunder, rain, hail, and snow—along with a break for sunshine—all within an hour. And in any season of the year.

Stand in a single mountain valley and watch the seasons change. It doesn't matter whether it's in the heart of the San Juans, or in the Indian Peaks, the Never Summers, in the Sangre de Cristos, or in a dozen other ranges. What a wonder to behold!

Autumn angling at Weller Lake  BRIAN BAILEY

Springtime in the Rockies is the season of surprises. Snowstorms can strike into June, and winter can hang on so long that springtime is merely an afterthought, a pause before summertime. There is no surprise so sweet as the first spring wind coursing through the pines. Sunshine melts the snow, streams run full, and cottonwoods and aspens bud into vibrant green. The delicate pasque flower pokes its way through the forest floor, acting like it's a pioneer of the plant world. As the season hits stride, tribes of flowers follow.

Down in the valleys it's calving season on the ranches. And high in the mountains it's lambing season for the bighorn sheep. Elk calves appear. Mule deer fawns gambol behind their mothers. Birds return from their tropical or Mexican vacations. Everywhere excitement stirs and a sense of something new fills the air.

In Colorado's high country, summer visits like a tourist, welcome and friendly but never able to stay for long. For the alpine animals, summer is no vacation at all. Never have I watched anything busier than a little creature called a pika. Summer is the season when these relatives of the rabbit must harvest grass for their winter meals, much like the ranchers of the lowlands store hay for their herds. One day I watched a pika hustle back and forth for an hour, transporting mouthfuls of grass from a nearby meadow to its rock-bound nest.

Summer reminds us of that fanciful question heard from one visitor: "So when do the deer grow up to be elk?" Never, of course, is the answer. But after tallying the magnitude of nature's productivity during a single Rocky Mountain summer, nothing seems impossible.

What I like best about a summer's day is its artistic creation of clouds. Mountains exert such power that they make their own weather. While a July morning begins clear, many times by noon the sky can be filling with armies of clouds. Nowhere does lightning appear to strike more often than on a summer afternoon in Colorado.

Autumn is Colorado's best-kept secret. September and October can be cloudless. Groves of aspen change from green to gold. The days are warm, the nights are crisp. Tourist haunts are uncrowded. There comes a relaxing of the spirit, a lull between the busy summer days and the advancing season of cold and snow.

Coloradans always know when autumn has come: the bull elk announce it. There exist other sounds in nature that strike a signal note of wildness, but none echo off the mountainsides with the same primeval pitch as that of the bull elk. The sound fills the valleys, and marks a season filled with urgency and preparation. Ahead lies a test of survival.

Soon I will scan the horizon and hear the hostile winds roar across the high peaks. How can anything survive in such a place in winter? In some valleys winter extends its icy clutches for six months or more. But the snow-capped peaks, if enjoyed from a cozy cabin or beheld on a frosty morning, give a gift of silence and beauty that is hard to forget.

The highest suspension bridge in the world, spanning the Royal Gorge near Canon City   JACK OLSON

When I dream of Colorado, the scenes that come to mind are gained from the mountaintops. Perhaps my memory and those views I treasure are enhanced by the magic of elevation and the clarity of mountain air. Perhaps it's all illusion. But there is nothing like those hard-won vistas seen from atop the peaks.

Mountains have a purpose. I hear people say, "That's my mountain," even though they don't own it. They go on to explain, "That's where we had our picnic, or that's where we saw the sheep, or that's where we went for a walk with grandpa."

I think Colorado has more mountain climbers than the rest of the United States combined. On the average summer's day, it's possible there are more hikers and mountaineers scrambling along ridges and summits than anywhere else on the globe, save Switzerland and Austria. There's also a strange obsession that strikes a growing number of Coloradans: to climb every mountain exceeding 14,000 feet in elevation. Once those fifty-odd peaks have been conquered, the compulsive climbers turn to summits of lesser stature, those rising above 13,000 feet.

Mountains are so powerful in Colorado that they can put perspective in a person's life. They can teach lessons, like humility or endurance or courage.

A friend of mine says Colorado's mountains are "user friendly." Lacking grizzly bears, a tangle of swamps or forests, and similar perils, these peaks can be a delight to explore. Like many Coloradans, I confess to being challenged by mountain peaks. But the true satisfaction, for me, is savoring the journey—the smell of pines along the forested slopes, the abundant wildlife that calls the mountains home.

I'm convinced these rocky ridges and lofty summits allow our imaginations a chance to roam. Here we encounter a few of nature's surprises, or hear the cry of ravens carried in the breeze, or gain some elevation in our spirit simply by ascending to those alpine regions. Mountains, I think, play an important part in the lives of Coloradans, providing a sense of permanence in an age when change confronts us daily. And mountains speak of power, sparking our creative forces, renewing our energy, and challenging us to test our limits.

Colorado can mean something different for everyone. To an avid skier it's a day under the clear blue sky in a deep bowl of powder at Winter Park, Keystone, or Vail. To a bicycle rider it's a day to conquer Independence Pass. To a horserider it's a trip into the Flat Tops Wilderness. To an urban adventurer, it's a day exploring the Denver Museum of Natural History. To a sports fan, it's an afternoon cheering on the Broncos or the Rockies. To a kayaker, it's a day on the Cache la Poudre or the Colorado River.

What Coloradans like best about their state is its variety. From the cosmopolitan delights of Denver to the rustic romance of a dude ranch. In Colorado it's possible to sample the wilderness, climb a mountain, go bicycling, eat at a fine restaurant, and attend an evening symphony concert—all in a single day.

For most people Colorado has always been a land of challenge, and of promise and optimism. Just ask the prospectors, or the grandchildren of homesteaders. Over the years Colorado has also cultivated its image as a land of pleasure. Just ask the resort owners or the horse wranglers.

What makes Colorado wonderful? Ask the park rangers. They might say it's the scenery or our chance to savor the remnants of wilderness. Or maybe they'll confess to having a special camping or fishing spot far up the canyon of the Cache la Poudre, a place only they and a few other Coloradans know about.

Ask someone who knows the forests, and they might describe a dramatic sight near Aspen: in the foreground lies placid Maroon Lake, its shores surrounded by groves of golden aspen, with snow-clad Maroon Bells towering in the distance. This is one of the most photographed spots in the West. Ask someone else, and they might mention the Mount of the Holy Cross or the Flat Top Wilderness, places less well-known but equally remarkable for natural beauty.

Ask someone in Monte Vista or Salida and they might tell you it isn't a place at all, it's a river, like the Arkansas, offering miles of wild waters for the pleasures of rafting and fishing. Ask a person who haunts Colorado's prairie lands and they might talk for hours about places you've never heard of, like the wonders of the Pawnee Buttes or the Picket Wire Canyon Lands, or something as simple as the predatory flight of a prairie falcon.

What I'm likely to remember most about Colorado are the good times and friendly faces. A great Mexican dinner in Walsenburg. An autumm stroll along Denver's Highline Canal. A summit victory celebration atop Longs Peak. Sampling the hospitality of small towns such as Lake George, Rustic, Grand Lake, and Fairplay. Or gazing at a glorious Rocky Mountain sunset.

Colorado is a place where dreams come true.

Curt Buchholtz,
Estes Park

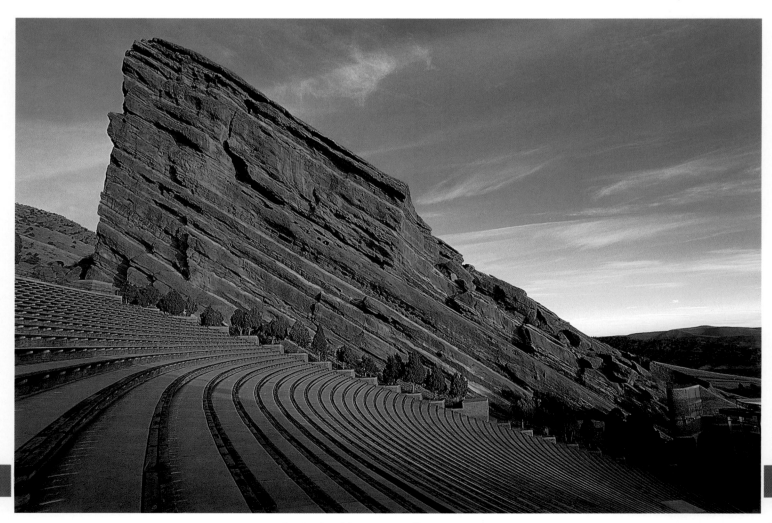

Red Rocks Ampitheater near Denver   ERIC WUNROW

Aspens ablaze with fall color on Kebler Pass near Crested Butte   ERIC WUNROW

*" The sky and the earth combine to form a Wonderland every evening—such rich, velvety coloring in crimson and violet . . . and then the glorious afterglow which seems to blend earth and heaven! For color, the Rocky Mountains beat all I have seen. "*

Isabella L. Bird,
A Lady's Life in the Rocky Mountains

Alpenglow on the Grenadier Mountains and Molas Lake south of Silverton  ERIC WUNROW

Majestic San Juan Mountains touching the clouds in southwestern Colorado   ERIC WUNROW

A splash of color on the flanks of Red Mountain in the San Juans   BRANSON REYNOLDS

*" The word 'Colorado' came from the Spanish adjective meaning 'red' or 'ruddy', but that word clearly does not do justice to yellows of the aspen, the green of the conifers, or the blue of the horizon. Simply put, Colorado is dramatic, its beauty is majestic and its vistas are endless. "*

former Governor Richard D. Lamm,
Colorado

Marcelina Mountain towers above 9,980-foot Kebler Pass in Gunnison County    JIM WARK

A forest mosaic in Maroon Creek Canyon near Aspen,
White River National Forest    JEFF GNASS

Fall foliage in the Mount Sneffels Wilderness with 13,496-foot Mears Peak towering above    ERIC WUNROW

An island of monkey flowers in Fraser Creek, Flat Tops Wilderness   WILLARD CLAY

*❝ The muscle in water comes from its fall, and with many rivers in Colorado dropping thousands of feet from headwaters to the border, the state's waters have plenty of muscle. ❞*

Jeff Rennicke,
The Rivers of Colorado

North Clear Creek Falls west of Denver in the Rio Grande National Forest   JOHN WARD

The Green River and the Gates of Lodore Canyon, Dinosaur National Monument   SCOTT T. SMITH

Gunnison River rushes through the Black Canyon of the Gunnison National Monument   WILLARD CLAY

Taking in the view from the 14,017-foot summit of Wilson Peak near Telluride   ERIC WUNROW

Fighting gravity on a 5.13 climb called "Evil" in Clear Creek Canyon west of Golden   STEWART M. GREEN

A lone bighorn ewe on 11,669-foot Guanella Pass
south of Georgetown   ERIC WUNROW

*" As long as there are mountains,
there will be romance in climbing
their challenging cliffs...or in merely
looking at their snow-capped peaks
from afar...or in just knowing that
they belong to you and me.* "

Carl Skiff,
The Majestic Fourteeners...
Colorado's Highest

" *Mountains define Colorado. The history of the state, both human and natural, is in great measure the history of mountains. Gold scratched out of mountainsides, elk making for a pass blown free of snow by the wind, skiers carving S-turns in powder, ragged edges of timberline ablaze with morning sun, slats of ghost towns creaking like the backs of miners who came and went—the personality of Colorado is mirrored in its mountains as clearly and as beautifully as the reflection of a peak in a still pond. Colorado is mountains.* "

Jeff Rennicke,
Colorado Mountain Ranges

Rugged mountains of the Gore Range reflected in ponds high in the White River National Forest   BRIAN LITZ

Storm clouds gathering above the sandstone cliffs of Colorado National Monument near Grand Junction    TOM TILL

❝ *In breadth of effect—in airy depth and expansion—in simple yet most majestic outline, and in originality yet exquisite harmony of color, this landscape is unlike anything I have ever seen.* ❞

Bayard Taylor,
Colorado: A Summer Trip

Solitary sentinel, Chimney Rock stands alone on the Ute Mountain Ute Reservation south of Cortez   JACK OLSON

A cold sea of winter clouds surrounds Independence Monument in Colorado   JOHN WARD

> **"** *Truly we have three seasons.... We have a burst of life, a long pause and then a few months of intermittent snow and arctic cold.* **"**

James Grafton Rogers,
My Rocky Mountain Valley

Mountain lion   SHERM SPOELSTRA

An abandoned mine tipple on Red Mountain, San Juans  DAVID BLANKENSHIP / NEW ENGLAND STOCK PHOTO

Remnants of the silver mining era on the Crystal River, upriver from Redstone   TOM TILL

*66* *Only yesterday it seems the valley was a street of mines. . . . Six-horse wagons rumbled to the railway from side canyons carrying gold and silver hidden in mud and rock just lifted from underground. Tremors from subterranean blasting shook dishes on breakfast and dinner tables. Miners in stained overalls and high rubber boots plodded at daybreak to the mine portals and wearily homeward at dusk.* *99*

James Grafton Rogers,
My Rocky Mountain Valley

High mountain peaks framed in the ruins of the ghost town Alta near Telluride   DAN PEHA

*“ In summer, as early as four in the morning, railroad buffs begin to clog the little orange depot, shivering in the predawn which will soon change to a hot and dusty day in Durango. The first train departs with a low and mournful whistle that still sends shivers up the backs of many who have lived in Durango all their lives. A cloud of soot erupts from the smokestack and as cameras click and children wave goodbye, the engineer blows the whistle again and number 'four-seventy-waterbag' is on its way down the yard-wide track to Silverton. ”*

Nancy Wood,
Colorado: Big Mountain Country

Stoking the fire on the Durango & Silverton Narrow Gauge
Railroad locomotive   DAN PEHA

Chugging along the Animas River on board the Durango & Silverton Narrow Gauge Railroad   ERIC WUNROW

A fine day for fishing in Routt National Forest near Steamboat Springs  DAVID EPPERSON

Angler's reward: a rainbow trout in the Frying Pan River near Basalt   R.E. BARBER

 

 

*  I hike and fish because it's pretty country and the trout are out there, with the red slashes on their jaws and their fine, efficient coloring that changes from lake to lake. I look for two things, mostly: trout and solitude, in that order.*

John Gierach,
Trout Bum

The Crystal River rushes past an old log cabin in the White River National Forest   MARK & JENNIFER MILLER

Sandstone cliffs crumble into the Dolores River, San Juan National Forest   SCOTT T. SMITH

Hoping to get lucky: fishing the South Platte River   R.E. BARBER

*« If a fisherman ever reaches the point where he can hook an eighteen-incher after landing a handful of small stockers and not be left in shock, if a fisherman could take a sixteen-incher from a small pocket in the trickle that is a small creek and not stand in stunned disbelief, if a person could stare at the quiet water of mid-river, line limp after the take, run, and subsequent loss of a sea-run mystery and not feel his heart pounding with the adrenaline rush of sudden surprise, then he ought to hang up his rod and waders forever. »*

Steven J. Meyers,
Notes from the San Juans

33

Little sunflowers, showy asters, and rosy paintbrush adorn an alpine meadow   KEN ARCHER

**"** *The entire region is a wild-flower garden. Bloom-time lasts all summer long. The scores of streams which splash down from the snows are fringed with ferns and blossoms. . . . Difference of altitude, topography, and moisture-distribution induce nearly a thousand varieties to bloom in and to color this glad wild garden.* **"**

Enos A. Mills,
The Spell of the Rockies

A baby porcupine smells a wild rose   R.E. BARBER

Rain-soaked skyrocket flowers below the lofty summits of Mount Crested Butte and Gothic Mountain   JACK W. DYKINGA

Rosy paintbrush and wild parsley on the banks of a mountain stream   KEN ARCHER

Vibrant summer colors of Indian paintbrush and lupine in Rio Grande National Forest   JACK W. DYKINGA

Remnants of the Anasazi cliff dwellings (AD 1000 to 1300) at Mesa Verde National Park   TOM TILL

> " *We could almost see them around us. We could watch them at work in the fields, with the dogs barking and the turkeys calling; the women busy at their looms or grinding corn for the midday meal; the children playing near. . . . With so much just as the people left it, it is almost impossible to reconcile ourselves to the mental awakening of finding nothing but silent walls before us.* "

Benjamin Alfred Wetherill,
The Wetherills of the Mesa Verde

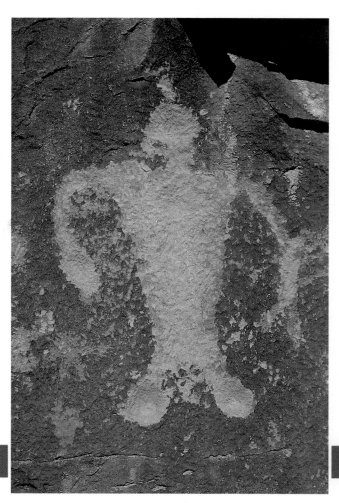

Petroglyph at Ute Mountain Tribal Park near Cortez
JACK OLSON

Indian tepee at sunset in Daniels Park    SHERM SPOELSTRA

66 *We need our songs. We need our dances. That's what makes us whole. As long as we have that we will always be here.* 99

July-Knight Frank,
Quoted in The Daily Sentinel

Young dancer of the Southern Ute tribe on the powwow trail
at Ignacio    BRANSON REYNOLDS

Ruins of Lowery Pueblo, built around AD 1000, northwest of Cortez    JACK OLSON

Sharing the fun of a Southern Ute tribal fair parade in Ignacio    JACK OLSON

Greater sandhill cranes at the Monte Vista Wildlife Refuge    KEN ARCHER

Mountain goat kids playing king of the boulder on
Mount Evans    SHERM SPOELSTRA

Bighorn rams in Rocky Mountain National Park   KEN ARCHER

*66 Wildlife is the heartbeat of the land. . . .It is the bighorn sheep and the ptarmigan that make the high country more than just rock and ice. It is the cloud of dust behind a running herd of pronghorns that makes the prairie more than empty horizons. And it is the song of the canyon wren that makes the canyons more than silent walls. 99*

Jeff Rennicke,
*Colorado Wildlife*

Irrigated field in the eastern plains near Greeley  ERIC WUNROW

Wheat fields stretch to the horizon in northeastern Colorado   STEPHEN L. RAMSEY

A farmer works a hayfield near Steamboat Springs   GLENN RANDALL

❝ *The land is most glorious in June. . . . there are fields of ripe, harvest-ready, picturebook golden wheat; stands of baby green corn or milo, foot-high, poking up tentative stalks and leaves from the bottoms of deep, wide irrigation furrows, furrows flooded with hundreds, sometimes thousands, of gallons of water per minute.* ❞

Jeff and Jessica Pearson,
No Time But Place

Feeding cattle in El Paso County   BOB BARRETT

Windmill on the Pawnee National Grassland in Weld County
SCOTT T. SMITH

The passing of a summer thunderstorm over a farm near Commerce City   ERIC WUNROW

Wheels of fortune created by circular irrigation sprinklers in the arid,
fertile San Luis Valley, Alamosa County   JIM WARK

East Pawnee Butte pierces the autumn sky in Pawnee National Grassland   SCOTT T. SMITH

Prairie sunset northeast of Fort Collins   LAURENCE PARENT

Doe and buck pronghorn antelope east of
Colorado Springs   KEN ARCHER

*"...the land of eastern Colorado
does not shout for attention; its
ornamentation is understated and spare.
Beauty is more likely to be defined by
quality of light, an engulfing stillness, or
surprising appearances of wildlife...."*

Alan S. Kesselheim,
Silhouette on a Wide Land

Sandstone cliffs at Garden of the Gods frame Pikes Peak in the background   LAURENCE PARENT

*He loved . . . Pikes Peak over all. This noble presidence, he knew, had always been the greatest of Rocky Mountain landmarks. . . . It was a kingdom in itself. . . .*

Marshall Sprague,
Newport in the Rockies

Pikes Peak's 14,110-foot summit dominates the skyline
west of Colorado Springs   MICHAEL S. SAMPLE

Dawn light on Cathedral Rock at 1,350-acre Garden of the Gods Park   ERIC WUNROW

Cathedral Spires, Pulpit Rock, and Three Graces of the
Garden of the Gods   ERIC WUNROW

*Near Colorado Springs . . . is located one of the most beautiful and curious little parks, . . . . Around these rocks, . . . according to the mythological stories of the people, the 'gods' found such lovely times in play that they christened it a garden.*

Henry T. Williams,
The Pacific Tourist

Civic Center Park in the Mile High City of Denver   JACK OLSON

**"** *Denver is much more than the capital of Colorado. It is, in a very full sense, Colorado's 'front office.'* **"**

George Sessions Perry,
"The Cities of America:
Denver"

The Basilica of Immaculate Conception in Denver
ERIC WUNROW

Denver Civic Center adorned with Christmas lights   STEVE MOHLENKAMP

U.S. Olympic Training Center in Colorado Springs   DAVE BLACK

Colorado Rockies baseball in Denver   DAVE BLACK

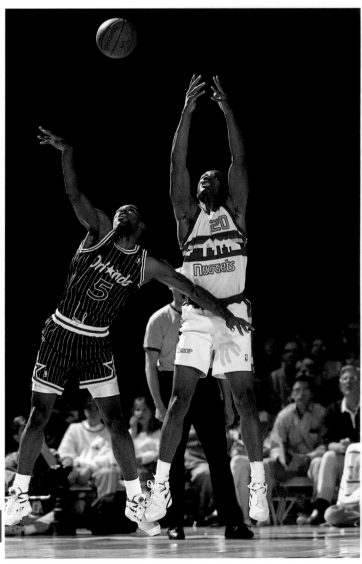

Denver Nuggets basketball   DAVE BLACK

Mile High Stadium, jubilant home of the Denver Broncos   PHIL LAURO

Broncos quarterback John Elway   DAVE BLACK

**66** *When I came here as a rookie . . . I thought all stadiums were alike, that fans everywhere were the same. But I found out there is a difference. No matter how many times I step onto the field, no matter how many times I hear the cheers, I get chills. . . .I can't imagine wanting to play anywhere else.* **99**

John Elway,
Denver Broncos Football

Chapel at the U.S. Air Force Academy    STEWART M. GREEN

Elegant Broadmoor Hotel in Colorado Springs    ERIC WUNROW

University of Colorado Boulder campus nestles against the foothills  JACK OLSON

Preserving the past in the Denver Museum of Natural History  PHIL LAURO

Lofty peaks of the Sangre de Cristo Range rise above Great Sand Dunes National Monument in the San Luis Valley   JAMES RANDKLEV

> *When you approach the valley's eastern edge, a large light-colored area up against the mountains catches your eye. Gold, brown, cream, gray, tan, even pink—the colors shift with the light, . . . . Finally, you draw near—close enough to discover one more of the contrasts held within the Colorado Rockies. For here mountain peaks drop in dark, jagged contours to meet the soft lines and uninterrupted colors of sand dunes.*

Stephen Trimble,
Great Sand Dunes

Dune surfing at Great Sand Dunes National Monument   WILLIAM R. SALLAZ

59

Winter storm clouds catch evening light over Molas Pass   MICHAEL S. SAMPLE

*66 We know of no country better worth the title of the 'Switzerland of America' than Colorado, with its beautiful mountain parks, valleys, and springs. Go and see them all. The tour will be worthy of remembrance for a life-time. 99*

Henry T. Williams,
The Pacific Tourist

Fireworks at Purgatory Ski Area near Durango   DAN PEHA

Snowcapped San Juan Mountains near Ridgway   ROD WALKER

Kids get a lift at Winter Park Ski Area   DAVE BLACK

Winter pasture in the Roaring Fork River Valley near Aspen   GALEN ROWELL

"On what fun..." Open sleigh ride through the mountain snow at
the C Lazy U Ranch near Granby   ROD WALKER

Skaters enjoy the cold, sunny winters in Grand County   ROD WALKER

Anglers undeterred by winter try their luck
at Elevenmile Canyon Reservoir   KEN ARCHER

Diamond face of 14,255-foot Longs Peak in Rocky Mountain National Park   ERIC WUNROW

*“ If a prophet were looking for a peak to retreat to, if a god were looking for a perch from which to toss thunderbolts at the people of the plains. . . .they surely would stride to the top of Longs Peak. ”*

Stephen Trimble,
Longs Peak

Climber enjoying evening light with Longs Peak in the distance
ERIC WUNROW

Columbine Falls below Longs Peak in Rocky Mountain National Park, the showpiece of Colorado's public recreational lands   GLENN RANDALL

Aerial view of the seemingly endless Mount Sneffels Wilderness Area, Uncompahgre National Forest   TOM TILL

> *Very little in the world can compare to the scenery of Colorado. The vistas here stretch the eyes, enlighten the heart, and make the spirit humble.... This is indeed the top of the nation.*

John Gunther,
Inside U.S.A.

Bald eagle, symbol of freedom and rugged individuality, in the Uncompahgre River valley   DANIEL J. COX

Splash of fall color on the rugged San Juan Mountains near Dolores   JIM WARK

Indian paintbrush and yucca on the plains near Parker   DAVID BLANKENSHIP / NEW ENGLAND STOCK PHOTO

Splendor of wildflowers near Thunder Lake, Rocky Mountain
National Park   GLENN RANDALL

*" From the eastern plains to the
mountain ranges of central Colorado and
on to the plateau and canyon country, the
intricate workings of natural forces have
combined to paint a landscape nearly
infinite in its variety. "*

Emerson Pearson,
The Hiker's Guide to Colorado

Elk, or wapiti, feeding on summer grass along a high mountain lake   R.E. BARBER

A wily and elusive bull elk peers from a hiding place in thick willow brush    KEN ARCHER

 

*“ Of all views of living things in the Rocky Mountains, a bull elk with half a dozen points on each antler, alert and listening . . . is the most imperial. His body scarcely stirs. His head shifts slowly, his nose sniffing, his eyes rolling, the forest of horns flicking in and out of the sun spots. Suddenly with a crash he is gone, splintering branches and shrubs. ”*

James Grafton Rogers,
My Rocky Mountain Valley

Oak brush and aspen trees donning fall colors near Paonia   JOHN WARD

**❝** *Conifers have a majestic monotony, like someone who is always right. . . . But aspen has éclat, a glorious brashness in defiance of the rules, the flapper who does the Charleston in the midst of the grand waltz. The landscape would be dull indeed without them.* **❞**

Ann Zwinger,
Beyond the Aspen Grove

Mule deer buck   TIM CHRISTIE

Aspen trees surrounded by cow parsnips in the West Elk Mountains, Gunnison National Forest  WILLARD CLAY

Palette of autumn colors revealed in aspen leaves   SCOTT T. SMITH

Town of Ouray, named in honor of Ute Indian Chief Ouray, sprawls at the foot of the San Juan Mountains   JEFF GNASS

Enjoying summer's sweet pleasures in Boulder   JACQUELYN HARP

Once a mining boom town, picturesque Telluride is now a popular resort    JEFF GNASS

Getting a helping hand in Boulder    JACQUELYN HARP

66 *Small towns are good because everything is simplified. The work, the gettin' there, goin' fishin' and huntin', goin' to church, savin' money, buildin' friendships and enjoyin' life. And after all that last one should be one of our main goals.* 99

Pete Smythe,
"Sweepin's from Smythe's General Store,
with Somethin' for the Daily Battle of Life"

Fireworks over Aspen during Winterskol celebration   CATHERINE L. DORAN / NEW ENGLAND STOCK PHOTO

13,300-foot Mount Daly looms over Snowmass Village   BRIAN BAILEY

Solo ice climber scaling partially frozen Ames Falls near Telluride   BRIAN BAILEY

Freestyle skiers taking to the air at Breckenridge Ski Area   PHIL LAURO

Bustling Vail Village during ski season   JACK OLSON

Powder skiing: the special gift between earth and sky   ROD WALKER

“ *Powder snow skiing...is a special gift of the relationship between earth and sky. It only comes in sufficient amounts in particular places, at certain times on this earth;...People devote their lives to it, 'for the pleasure of being so purely played' by gravity and snow.* ”

Dolores LaChapelle,
Earth Wisdom

Snow boarder "shredding" a slope laden in new snow   BRIAN BAILEY

Winter sunrise on Big Thompson River in Moraine Park, Rocky Mountain National Park    WILLARD CLAY

❝ *Winter, for some people, is the most beautiful time in the mountains. Between blizzards, when the sky clears and the wind drops, and the mountain light gives a fine blue transparency to the shadows between the drifts, the landscape seems wonderfully benign.* ❞

Bryce S. Walker,
The Great Divide

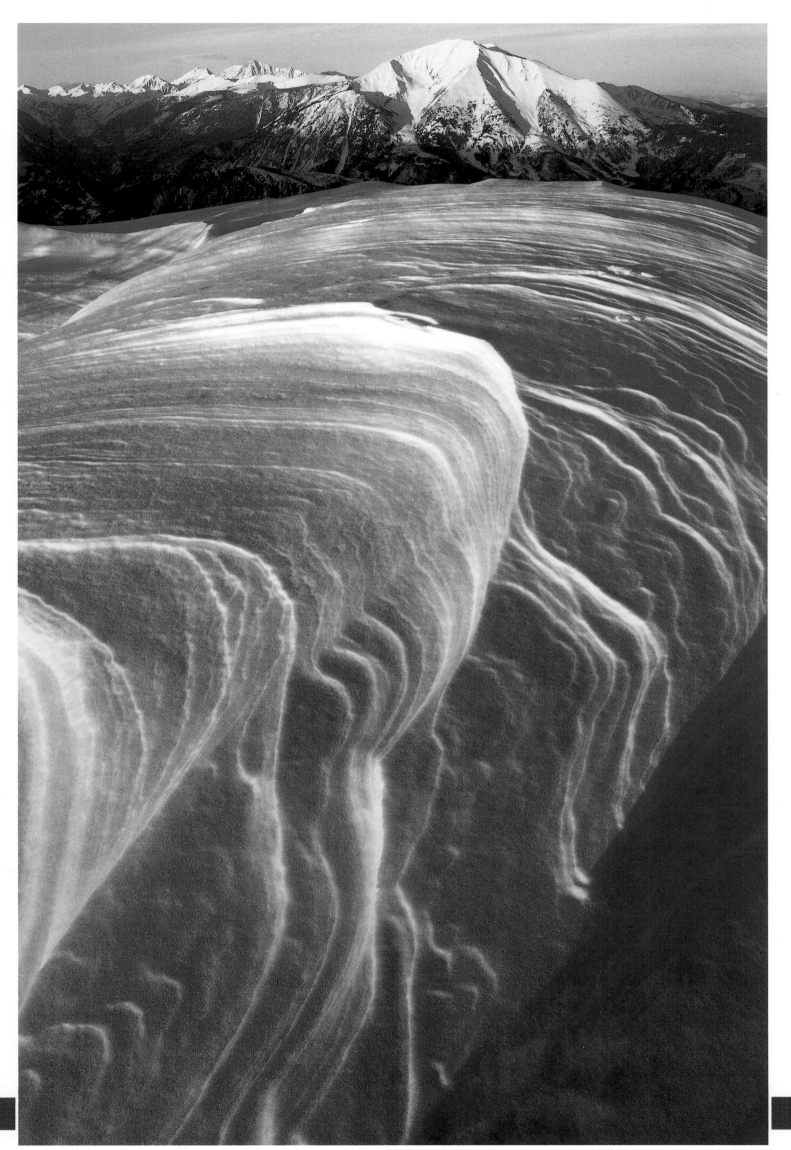

Wind-sculpted snow drifts on Compass Mountain in the Elk Mountains   STACY OLSON

Green River meanders through Browns Park National Wildlife Refuge in northwestern Colorado    SCOTT T. SMITH

*" The rivers of Colorado have scrawled the signature of life across the state's landscape, in the etchings of their deep canyons, in the splatter of green wheat fields, in the rings of willow stumps, in the huts of beavers, and in the footprints of human history. Life in Colorado is indeed written in water, and its signature is the rivers. "*

Jeff Rennicke,
The Rivers of Colorado

Canada goose preening    KEN ARCHER

Marshes along Rio Grande State Wildlife Area   TOM TILL

Mallard drake tipping to feed   KEN ARCHER

Sandhill cranes at sunrise on the Monte Vista Wildlife Refuge near Alamosa    BRANSON REYNOLDS

Great blue heron    MICHAEL S. SAMPLE

Sunset over an alpine tarn in San Isabel National Forest   WILLARD CLAY

Pond along East Dallas Creek below Mount Sneffels, Uncompahgre National Forest   WILLARD CLAY

*❝ It is snow that makes a river in Colorado, not spring rains or summer thunderstorms. ❞*

Jim Carrier,
Down the Colorado

Chorus frog   KEN ARCHER

Beaver ponds surrounded by mountain grandeur in the Elk Mountains, White River National Forest   MICHAEL S. SAMPLE

Bull moose   MICHAEL S. SAMPLE

*66 Colorado is a land shaped by water. Long ago, glacial ice carved the face of the state, slicing mountains, cutting canyons, and gouging wide valleys. Today, the waters of rivers, creeks, lakes, ponds, and wetlands give shape to the land around them. 99*

Jeff Rennicke,
Colorado Wildlife

Lupine and Indian paintbrush bask in the sun atop Grand Mesa near Grand Junction   TOM TILL

" *Colorado scenery combined with such a glorious climate, at last 'enthused' me, . . . . The very sense of living was an absolute delight which can not be realized by those who have never experienced the buoyancy of this electric air.* "

Emily Faithful,
Three Visits to America

91

Richardson's ground squirrel  SHERM SPOELSTRA

Bouquet of columbines and thistles amid boulders in the Collegiate Peaks Wilderness, San Isabel National Forest   WILLARD CLAY

*To us there came also a wayside greeting more beautiful than the clouds, bluer than the sky, and gladder than the sun,—only a flower, one flower! But it was the Rocky Mountain columbine,—peerless among columbines, wondrous among flowers.*

Helen Hunt Jackson,
Bits of Travel at Home

Rocky Mountain columbines, the state flower, flourish in Yankee Boy Basin, San Juan Range    WILLARD CLAY

Aspen trees frame a mountain scene in Gunnison National Forest near Crested Butte   JAMES RANDKLEV

Black bear cub smelling spring flowers in the foothills east of the Continental Divide   PERRY CONWAY

Alpine asters in Uncompahgre National Forest   JACK OLSON

*" In Colorado, high upon the spine of North America, one has a keen sense of the original earth, of its deep, definitive life. "*

N. Scott Momaday,
Colorado

An outfitter leading hunters into the backcountry of the La Plata Mountains   BRANSON REYNOLDS

Running along the shore of Haynach Lake in Rocky Mountain National Park   GLENN RANDALL

Trekking with llamas in the Maroon Bells–Snowmass Wilderness Area near Aspen RICK SCHAFER

High altitude mountain biking in Pitkin County BRIAN BAILEY

*" To feel the wind in your face; . . . to feel the cold of dawn nip your ears and the heat of noon burn your back; to hear the thunder of the Colorado and the roar of mountain streams, . . . all this is to grow young again. "*

Zane Grey,
Picturesque America

Shooting rapids on the Arkansas River, downriver from Salida   JACK OLSON

Paragliding over the Elk Mountains   BRIAN BAILEY

Up, up, and away: The Snowmass Balloon Festival  GALEN ROWELL

Speed and grace of team roping at Keystone Resort   PHIL LAURO

Saddle bronc action at the Colorado State Fair in Pueblo   DAVE BLACK

Eight seconds of bull riding excitement   RANDY KALISEK / F-STOCK

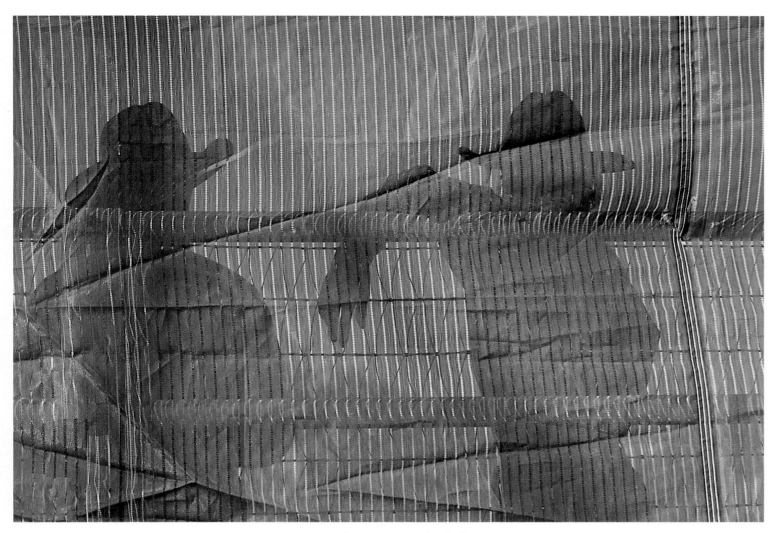

Cowboys taking a break from rodeo action in Durango    DAN PEHA

Little Britches Rodeo fashion in Delta    WILLIAM SALLAZ

*66 They wore cowboy boots creased to the shape of their feet and the angle of their stirrups. Their belts were hand-tooled leather. The silver buckles were designed with a monogram or with the name of a county rodeo won with the skill they had spent their lives acquiring. 99*

Nancy Wood,
Colorado: Big Mountain Country

Hispanic folk dancer at Cinco de Mayo celebration in Colorado Springs   STEWART M. GREEN

Bent's Old Fort, founded in 1869 at the junction of the Arkansas and Purgatoire rivers near La Junta   JACK OLSON

Covered wagon at Bent's Old Fort, the most important stop on the mountain section
of the Santa Fe Trail   TOM TILL

> *The clarity of light confuses one's sense of scale. Faraway mountains are so sharp in outline that they seem much closer. The intense brightness of the light is untempered by large shadows, large buildings, or large trees. It bathes the mountains and creates a dazzling luculent landscape.*

Ann H. Zwinger and Beatrice E. Willard,
Land Above the Trees

Pika in Rocky Mountain National Park    BRANSON REYNOLDS

Vibrant light and a rainbow over the ghostly mining camp remains of Animas Forks  JOHN WARD

Mount Champion Mill at Halfmoon Creek, San Isabel National Forest   JOHN WARD

*" There must be lots of ghosts up there on those high, cold peaks. . . . Those grubby, grinning old ghosts must be just sitting up there. . . talking still about the price of silver. . .and about the way it used to be. . . way back in those frantic, hard-living, hard-fighting, often-tragic, often-bleak. . .but always good old days. "*

Carl Akers,
Carl Akers' Colorado

Remnants of the Silver Pick Mine below Mount Wilson   ERIC WUNROW

Miner's cabin in the mountains above Aspen   DAVID BLANKENSHIP / NEW ENGLAND STOCK PHOTO

19th Century architecture in downtown Leadville   MARK & JENNIFER MILLER

Erosion-sculpted volcanic tuff crowned by Englemann spruce in the La Garita Wilderness near Creede   JACK W. DYKINGA

Sandstone mounds called the Coke Ovens at Colorado National Monument near Grand Junction   SCOTT T. SMITH

Cutthroat Castle ruins amid sagebrush in Hovenweep National Monument west of Cortez
MARK & JENNIFER MILLER

The Colorado River flowing through Ruby Canyon on Utah-Colorado border west of Grand Junction    TOM TILL

    **❝** *The Colorado is an outlaw. It belongs only to the ancient, eternal earth. As no other, it is savage and unpredictable of mood, peculiarly American in character. It has for its background the haunting sweep of illimitable horizons, the immensities of unbroken wilderness. From perpetually snow-capped peaks to stifling deserts below sea level, it cuts the deepest and truest cross section through the continent.* **❞**

Frank Waters,
The Colorado

Big Thompson River at Spruce Creek, Rocky Mountain National Park   JOHN WARD

Water ouzel or dipper   MICHAEL S. SAMPLE

Niagara Peak looms behind deserted mine buildings at Animas Forks    ERIC WUNROW

Badger emerges from its winter den    SHERM SPOELSTRA

Mountain goat nanny and kid on Mount Evans   KEN ARCHER

Alpine bluebells below the Castles, West Elk Wilderness Area near Gunnison   JAMES RANDKLEV

Snowdon Peak from Molas Pass in the San Juan Mountains near Silverton   LARRY ULRICH

*" Even now, after 12 years of photographing in these mountains, I am still left with the empty feeling of not being able to put it all on film. It's simply too big, too wonderful, too beautiful. Surely the mountains reveal part of God's glory and nature to us. "*

David Lissy,
Colorado Ski!

Sunrise vista from Grand View, Colorado National Monument   JEFF GNASS

A dunes camp in Great Sand Dunes National Monument,
San Luis Valley   ERIC WUNROW

Chinese Wall in Flat Tops Wilderness northeast of Glenwood Springs   STACY OLSON

# *they made it possible*

*Oregon on My mind* would have been impossible to produce without the keen eyes and technical skills of more than thirty professional photographers. These men and women submitted their finest images, and the result shows in this stunning collection of photos. What does not show is the work it took to get these images—the early mornings to capture the sunrise, the long climbs through rugged terrain, the endless hours of waiting for the perfect light, the hundreds of shots that didn't turn out quite right, and the high level of technical skills that were aquired through years of experience and study. To all the photographers who contributed to *Oregon on My Mind*, we say thanks. We appreciate their art and their hard work.

Michael S. Sample and Bill Schneider
Publishers

## Photographers in *Oregon on My Mind*

Donna Ikenberry Aitkenhead

Wayne Aldridge

Mike Belozer

Charlie Boreland

Willard Clay

R. M. Collins III

Terry Donnelly

Brian Drake

Gerry Ellis

Dennis Frates

Larry Geddis

Jeff Gnass

Jon Gnass

David Jensen

Donald M. Jones

Gary Ladd

Russell Lamb

Tom & Pat Leeson

Wayne Michael Lottinville

J. C. Miller

Steve Mohlenkamp

Brian O'Keefe

Barry Peril

Bryan Peterson

Fred Pflughoft

Sue Pflughoft

Galen Rowell

Rick Schafer

Ty Smedes

Alan D. St. John

Gary Tarleton

Steve Terrill

Greg Vaughn

Steve Wanke

Kerry Wetzel

George Wuerthner

Art Wolfe

Jim Yuskavitch

Boreland Stock Photo

N.E. Stock Photo

Copyright © 1995 by Falcon®Publishing, Inc. Helena, Montana

All rights reserved, including the right to reproduce any part of this book in any form, except brief quotations for reviews, without the written permission of the publisher.

Design, typesetting, and other prepress work by Falcon Publishing, Helena, Montana. Printed in Korea.

Library of Congress Number: 94-71772

ISBN 1-56044-307-3

For extra copies of this book please check with your local bookstore, or write to Falcon, P.O. Box 1718, Helena, MT 59624 or call toll-free 1-800-582-2665.

Title page:
   Sunrise from Lookout Point   DENNIS FRATES
End papers:
   Ponderosa forest   FRED PFLUGHOLF

# *acknowledgments*

The publisher gratefully acknowledges the following sources:

Page 8 from *A Lady's Life In The Rocky Mountains* by Isabella L. Bird. Copyright © 1960 by University of Oklahoma Press, Publishing Division of the University, Norman, Oklahoma

Page 11 from *Colorado* by Craig Aurness and Richard D. Lamm. Copyright © 1986 by Boulton Publishing Services Inc., Toronto.

Page 14, 84 from *The Rivers of Colorado* by Jeff Rennicke. Copyright © 1985 by Falcon Press Publishing Co., Inc., Billings and Helena, Montana.

Page 19 from *The Majestic Fourteeners . . . Colorado's Highest* by Carl Skiff. Copyright © 1977 by Sundance Publications, Ltd., Silverton, Colorado

Page 20 from *Colorado Mountain Ranges* by Jeff Rennicke. Copyright © 1986 by Falcon Press Publishing Co., Inc., Billings and Helena, Montana.

Page 22 from *Colorado: A Summer Trip* by Bayard Taylor. Copyright © 1989 by the University Press of Colorado, Niwot, Colorado.

Page 25, 27, 71 from *My Rocky Mountain Valley* by James Grafton Rogers. Copyright © 1968 by James Grafton Rogers; Pruett Press, Inc., Boulder, Colorado.

Page 28, 101 from *Colorado: Big Mountain Country* by Nancy Wood. Copyright © 1969 by Myron Wood and Nancy Wood; Doubleday & Company, Inc., Garden City, New York.

Page 31 from *Trout Bum* by John Gierach. Copyright © 1986 by John Gierach; Pruett Publishing Company, Boulder, Colorado.

Page 33, 120 from *Notes from the San Juans: Thoughts About Fly Fishing and Home* by Stephen J. Meyers. Copyright © 1992 by Stephen J. Meyers; Lyons & Burford, Publishers, New York.

Page 35 from *The Spell of the Rockies* by Enos A. Mills. Copyright © 1911 by Enos A. Mills; Houghton Mifflin Company, Boston and New York.

Page 39 from *The Wetherills of the Mesa Verde: Autobiography of Benjamin*

*Alfred Wetherill* by Benjamin Alfred Wetherill. Edited and annotated by Maurine S. Fletcher. Copyright © 1977 by Maurine S. Fletcher; University of Nebraska Press, Lincoln.

Page 40 from "Powwow celebrates 3 tribes' traditions" in *The Daily Sentinel*, April 25, 1993.

Page 43, 89 from *Colorado Wildlife* by Jeff Rennicke. Copyright © 1990 by Falcon Press Publishing Co., Inc., Helena and Billings, Montana. Text copyright © 1990 by the Colorado Division of Wildlife.

Page 45 from *No Time But Place, A Prairie Pastoral* by Jeff and Jessica Pearson. Copyright © 1980 by Jeffery G. Pearson and Jessica S. Pearson; McGraw-Hill Book Company, New York. Published in association with San Francisco Book Company.

Page 49 from *Silhouette On A Wide Land* by Alan S. Kesselheim: Copyright © 1992 by Alan S. Kesselheim; Fulcrum Publishing, Golden, Colorado.

Page 50 from *Newport in the Rockies: The Life and Good Times of Colorado Springs* by Marshall Sprague. Copyright © 1961, 1971, 1980 by Marshall Sprague; Sage Books, Swallow Press, Chicago.

Page 51, 60 from *The Pacific Tourist* by Henry T. Williams. Copyright © 1876 by Henry T. Williams; Henry T. Williams, Publisher, New York.

Page 52 from "The Cities of America: Denver" by George Sessions Perry. Published in *The Saturday Evening Post*, August 24, 1946.

Page 55 from *Denver Broncos Football, Game Day Images*. Copyright © 1993 by the Denver Broncos Football Club and Walsworth Publishing Company, Kansas City, Missouri.

Page 59 from *Great Sand Dunes: the shape of the wind* by Stephen A. Trimble. Copyright © 1975 by Southwest Parks and Monuments Association, Globe, Arizona.

Page 64 from *Longs Peak: A Rocky Mountain Chronicle* by Stephen A. Trimble. Copyright © 1984 by Rocky Mountain Nature Association, Estes Park, Colorado.

Page 67 from *Inside U.S.A.* by John Gunther. Copyright © 1946, 1947, 1951 by John Gunther. Copyright © 1947 by

The Curtis Publishing Company; Harper and Row Publishers Incorporated, New York.

Page 69 from *The Hiker's Guide to Colorado* by Caryn and Peter Boddie. Copyright © 1991 by Falcon Press Publishing Co., Inc., Helena and Billings, Montana.

Page 73 from *Beyond the Aspen Grove* by Ann Zwinger. Copyright © 1970 by Ann Zwinger; Random House, New York.

Page 77 from "Sweepin's from Smythe's General Store, with Somthin' for the Daily Battle of Life" by Pete Smythe. Copyright © 1987? by Pete Smythe; The East Tincup Printery, Littleton, Colorado.

Page 80 from *Earth Wisdom* by Dolores LaChapelle. Copyright © 1978 by Dolores LaChapelle; The Guild of Tutors Press, Los Angeles, California.

Page 82 from *The Great Divide* by Bryce S. Walker. Copyright © 1973 by Time Inc.; Time-Life Books, New York.

Page 88 from *Down the Colorado: Travels on a Western Waterway* by Jim Carrier. Copyright © 1989 by the Denver Post Corporation; Roberts Rinehart, Inc. Publishers, Boulder, Colorado.

Page 91 from *Three Visits to America* by Emily Faithful. American edition, copyright © 1884 by Fowler & Wells Company, New York.

Page 92 from *Bits of Travel at Home* by Helen Hunt Jackson. Copyright © 1878 by Roberts Brothers; University Press: John Wilson & Son, Cambridge.

Page 95 from *Colorado: Summer/Fall/ Winter/Spring* by N. Scott Momaday. Copyright © 1973 by Rand McNally & Company, Chicago.

Page 97 from *Picturesque America: It's Parks and Playgrounds* edited by John Francis Kane. Copyright © 1925 by J. F. Kane; Resorts and Playgrounds of America, New York.

Page 104 from *Land Above the Trees: A Guide to American Alpine Tundra* by Ann H. Zwinger and Beatrice E. Willard, Ph.D. Copyright © 1972 by Ann H. Zwinger and Beatrice E. Willard; Harper & Row, Publishers, Inc., New York.

Page 106 from *Carl Akers' Colorado* by Carl Akers. Copyright © 1975 by The Old Army Press, Fort Collins, Colorado.

Page 110 from *The Colorado* by Frank Waters. Copyright © 1946 by Frank Waters; Holt, Rinehart and Winston, New York.

Page 115 from *Colorado Ski!* by David Lissy. Copyright © 1988 by Westcliffe Publishers, Inc., Englewood, Colorado.

---

### About Curt Buchholtz

Curt Buchholtz wrote the introduction to *Colorado on My Mind*. He is the Executive Director of the Rocky Mountain Nature Association and has written several books, including *Rocky Mountain National Park: A History*, and historical books on both Mesa Verde and the town of Littleton, Colorado. A twenty-five year resident of Colorado, he lives in Estes Park.

A cowboy near Steamboat Springs  LARRY PIERCE

" *I'm not sure that finding gold is so terribly important. It's the looking that matters. A person can do worse than spend the summers tramping about the mountains with horses, fishing for trout, scrambling the peaks, whether or not you ever find gold. Sometimes you fill your hat with something other than what you were looking for and that something other is even better.* "

Steven J. Meyers,
Notes from the San Juans